D0934289

BIG PICTURE 📷 SPORTS

Meet the
PHILADELPHIA EAGLES

BY
ZACK BURGESS

NORWOODHOUSE 🏠 PRESS

CHICAGO, ILLINOIS

NORWOOD HOUSE 🏠 PRESS

P.O. Box 316598 • Chicago, Illinois 60631
For more information about Norwood House Press please visit our website at
www.norwoodhousepress.com or call 866-565-2900.

Photo Credits:
   All photos courtesy of Associated Press, except for the following: Bowman Gum Co. (6, 10 top),
   Black Book Archives (7, 15, 18, 23), Fleer Corp. (10 bottom, 11 bottom),
   Hostess Brands/Wonder Bread (11 top), Topps, Inc. (11 middle), Sports Radio 94 WYSP (22).

   Cover Photo: Tom DiPace/Associated Press

   The football memorabilia photographed for this book is part of the authors' collection. The collectibles used
   for artistic background purposes in this series were manufactured by many different card companies—
   including Bowman, Donruss, Fleer, Leaf, O-Pee-Chee, Pacific, Panini America, Philadelphia Chewing Gum,
   Pinnacle, Pro Line, Pro Set, Score, Topps, and Upper Deck—as well as several food brands, including
   Crane's, Hostess, Kellogg's, McDonald's and Post.

Designer: Ron Jaffe
Series Editors: Mike Kennedy and Mark Stewart
Project Management: Black Book Partners, LLC.
Editorial Production: Lisa Walsh

LIBRARY OF CONGRESS CATALOGING-IN-PUBLICATION DATA
       Names: Burgess, Zack.
       Title: Meet the Philadelphia Eagles / by Zack Burgess.
       Description: Chicago, Illinois : Norwood House Press, [2016] | Series: Big
          picture sports | Includes bibliographical references and index. |
          Audience: Grade: K to Grade 3.
       Identifiers: LCCN 2015023112| ISBN 9781599537344 (Library Edition : alk.
          paper) | ISBN 9781603578370 (eBook)
       Subjects: LCSH: Philadelphia Eagles (Football team)--Miscellanea--Juvenile
          literature.
       Classification: LCC GV956.P44 B87 2016 | DDC 796.332/640974811--dc23
       LC record available at http://lccn.loc.gov/2015023112

288N—072016
Manufactured in the United States of America in North Mankato, Minnesota

CONTENTS

Words in **bold type** are defined on page 24.

The Eagles celebrate a big play.

CALL ME AN EAGLE

The eagle uses surprise and speed to capture its prey. The Philadelphia Eagles play the same way. Eagles fans love when the team snatches a victory late in a game. Nothing is more fun than watching their Eagles soar.

TIME MACHINE

The Eagles played their first season in 1933. The team won its first National Football League (NFL) championship 15 years later. Some of the most exciting players in NFL history have starred for the Eagles. **Steve Van Buren** and Randall Cunningham were two of the best.

STEVE VAN BUREN

Randall Cunningham signals to the sideline.

"Green" is the favorite color at the Eagles' stadium.

Best Seat in the House

The Eagles play their home games in a stadium just south of downtown Philadelphia. The stadium was built to protect the environment. Much of the energy it uses comes from the sun and the wind.

SHOE BOX

The trading cards on these pages show some of the best Eagles ever.

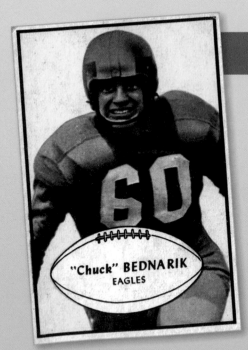

"Chuck" BEDNARIK
EAGLES

CHUCK BEDNARIK

LINEBACKER & CENTER • 1949-1962
In the early days of football, players stayed on the field for offense and defense. Chuck was the NFL's last "60-Minute Man."

TOMMY MCDONALD

RECEIVER • 1957-1963
Tommy was one of the NFL's smallest players. He used his quickness and soft hands to become one of the league's best receivers.

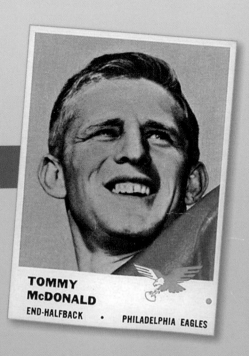

TOMMY McDONALD
END-HALFBACK • PHILADELPHIA EAGLES

BILL BERGEY

LINEBACKER · 1974-1980

Bill was an **All-Pro** in his first two seasons with the team. He led the Eagles to the Super Bowl in his last.

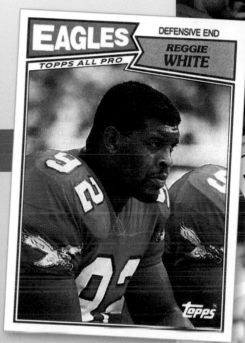

REGGIE WHITE

DEFENSIVE END · 1985-1992

Reggie was a terrifying pass-rusher. He had 124 **quarterback sacks** with the Eagles.

DONOVAN MCNABB

QUARTERBACK · 1999-2009

Donovan was a dangerous passer and runner. He guided the Eagles to the Super Bowl in 2005.

11

THE BIG PICTURE

Look at the two photos on page 13. Both appear to be the same. But they are not. There are three differences. Can you spot them?

Answers on page 23.

13

TRUE OR FALSE?

Brian Dawkins was a star defender. Two of these facts about him are **TRUE**. One is **FALSE**. Do you know which is which?

1 Brian was the first NFL player to force 30 fumbles and also have 30 **interceptions**.

2 Brian's nickname was the "Dawk Knight."

3 Brian decorated his locker with pictures and action figures of the X-Men character Wolverine.

Answer on page 23.

Brian Dawkins looks fierce.

15

It's selfie time for the Eagles and their fans!

16

Go Eagles, Go!

The people of Philadelphia truly believe the Eagles are fighting for the city's pride. One summer, the team offered tryouts to local players. A 30-year-old bartender named Vince Papale made the team. His story became a movie called *Invincible*.

ON THE MAP

Here is a look at where five Eagles were born, along with a fun fact about each.

 CHARLE YOUNG · FRESNO, CALIFORNIA
Charle made the **Pro Bowl** in his first three seasons with the Eagles.

 PETE RETZLAFF · ELLENDALE, NORTH DAKOTA
Pete was voted the NFL's best player in 1965.

 WILBERT MONTGOMERY · GREENVILLE, MISSISSIPPI
Wilbert once scored four touchdowns in one game.

 DAVID AKERS · LEXINGTON, KENTUCKY
David scored the most points in team history.

 STEVE VAN BUREN · LA CEIBA, HONDURAS
Steve led the NFL in rushing yards four times during the 1940s.

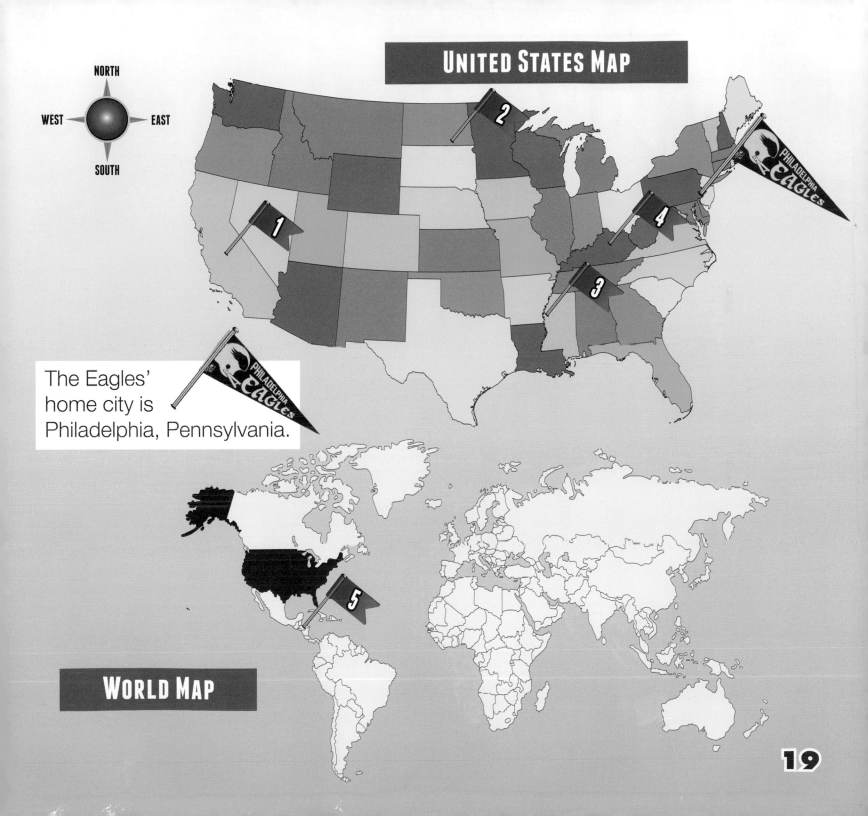

NORTH

WEST · EAST

SOUTH

UNITED STATES MAP

2

1

4

3

PHILADELPHIA
EAGLES

The Eagles'
home city is
Philadelphia, Pennsylvania.

5

WORLD MAP

Jordan Matthews wears the Eagles' home uniform.

Football teams wear different uniforms for home and away games. The main colors of the Eagles are dark green and white. For many years, they used a lighter shade of green.

Connor Barwin wears the Eagles' away uniform.

The Eagles' helmet is dark green. Silver and white wings spread from the middle across both sides. The team has used this design for more than 50 years.

WE WON!

In the years before the Super Bowl started, the Eagles won three NFL championships. They came in 1948, 1949, and 1960. The Eagles have also made it to the Super Bowl twice. Coach Dick Vermeil led them to the big game in 1980. They returned in 2004 under **Andy Reid**.

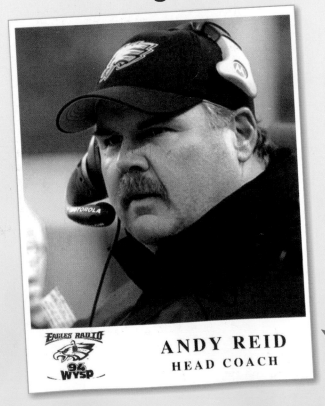

ANDY REID
HEAD COACH

RECORD BOOK

These Eagles set team records.

TOUCHDOWN PASSES		RECORD
Season:	Sonny Jurgensen (1961)	32
Career:	Donovan McNabb	216

TOUCHDOWN CATCHES		RECORD
Season:	Terrell Owens (2004)	14
Career:	Harold Carmichael	79

RUSHING YARDS		RECORD
Season:	**LeSean McCoy** (2013)	1,607
Career:	LeSean McCoy	6,792

ANSWERS FOR THE BIG PICTURE
#32 changed to #33, the stripe on #3's pants changed to gray, and the number on jersey #62 disappeared.

ANSWER FOR TRUE AND FALSE
#2 is false. Brian's nickname was not the "Dawk Knight."

Football Words

All-Pro
An honor given to the best NFL player at each position.

Interceptions
Passes caught by a defensive player.

Pro Bowl
The NFL's annual all-star game.

Quarterback Sacks
Tackles of the quarterback that lose yardage.

Index

Photos are on **BOLD** numbered pages.

About the Author

Zack Burgess has been writing about sports for more than 20 years. He has lived all over the country and interviewed lots of All-Pro football players, including Brett Favre, Eddie George, Jerome Bettis, Shannon Sharpe, and Rich Gannon. Zack was the first African American beat writer to cover Major League Baseball when he worked for the *Kansas City Star*.

About the Eagles

Learn more at these websites:

www.philadelphiaeagles.com • www.profootballhof.com

www.teamspiritextras.com/Overtime/html/eagles.html